HOW TO ESTIMATE REPAIR COSTS ON A REHAB

A Simple System for Successful Repair
Estimates as A Real Estate Investor

By

Jeff Leighton

Important Disclaimers

Table of Contents

Author's Note

———◆———

This book contains additional resources that I use on a daily basis as a real estate investor. Since I could not physically include these in the book, they are all available to download for free on my website **www.jeff-leighton.com**. That includes my repair estimator which is referenced several times in this guide, a deal analyzer, example contracts, marketing pieces that I use, recommended resources, helpful videos, and much more.

Introduction

Dear friend,

Welcome to *How To Estimate Repair Costs On A Rehab*. This guide was created to make it easier for you as a real estate investor to properly estimate repairs with real numbers and no fluff. Each section gives you valuable information on evaluating repairs, including one part with actual real-life estimates that you can use today and the exact repair estimator that I use.

If you are a looking for a 5-hour manual on real estate estimating with fancy diagrams and blueprints, then this is probably not for you.

However, if you are looking for a no-fluff, straight-to-the-good-stuff training on how to estimate repairs for your rehabs, then you are in the right place. This book is mostly for newer investors, although I truly believe any level of investor can gain value from this book.

When I was getting started as a real estate investor, there was no training guide like this. I either had to buy a $50, 2000-page book on construction best practices written in contractor language or I had to search the internet and forums to find out how much different repairs cost. Neither of those were good options, so that is where this book comes into play.

Why should you listen to me? I make six figures per year as a real estate investor and have been mentored by some of the top real estate investors in the world. I'm not saying that to brag, but instead to give you an idea of where my advice is coming from.

A word of note. Because of the different prices in each respective market, I give low estimates as well as high estimates, so you will have to adjust accordingly to your area.

Moreover, this book is not for houses over a million dollars. Once you get over a million, the level of finishes, size of the rehab, and other factors can be drastically different from a house below 1 million.

This book will help you become a savvier real estate investor because you'll gain a better understanding of renovations and estimates. We will also go over how to find the best contractors, the best renovations you can do in terms of ROI, and mistakes to avoid.

I try to share stories from my own experiences throughout this book so that you can get a real-world version of it too.

I am looking forward to sharing my knowledge with you, so let's jump into it.

7 Things You Should Know About Estimating Repairs

Before we jump into real-life estimates of all the components of a house, I want to go over seven general ideas when it comes to estimating repairs. This will help you better understand the real estate investing business and how much you should budget.

1. For starters, not every house will need a full gut renovation. You need to get a good sense of what the comps have been selling for and what condition those properties sell in.

    Sometimes the highest-selling properties are

not fully renovated; they are just in good livable condition. In that scenario, it would be riskier to do a full-scale renovation and try to set a neighborhood record for price.

Instead, you should do the sufficient repairs to bring it up to the comps, and perhaps slightly above the comps so that it stands out.

I've seen investors simply trash out the property, fix up the landscaping, and re-list the house a week or two later since the numbers still worked. Always keep the comps in mind when it comes to the scale of your renovation.

You don't always need to do a full-scale renovation unless the other sales in the neighborhood have been fully renovated.

2. Next, we have the old debate of being the project manager yourself or hiring a general contractor. Unless the job is small, I almost always prefer to hire a general contractor, even though there are pros and cons to each.

If you come from a construction background, then you could save some money by overseeing the project yourself and hiring out the different HVAC, electrical, plumbing, and other contractors that are needed. General contractors usually cost around 10% more.

That being said, if you can find a good general contractor, they can save you a lot of time and headache since they will essentially be your project manager. In a later section of this guide, we go over how to find the best contractors.

You will still have to oversee them and make sure they are hitting their timelines and cost estimates, but it should save you some time so that you can find more properties.

3.   The third thing to keep in mind is the area you live in and the finishes that are required in that specific area. One neighborhood versus another neighborhood can be drastically different.

In an area where homes sell over a million, a full kitchen might be 40 or 50K, while in another part of town a kitchen could be as little as 10K.

You want to look at the comps to make sure you are not overdoing it or underdoing it for your specific area.

The great thing about real estate, though, is that nowadays all the comp information on previous sales in your neighborhood are available online on sites like Redfin, Zillow, and others and include pictures of the properties and their level of finishes.

Study the comps online so that you know what level of renovation you will need to do. You can also get great ideas for what types of renovations to do by looking at past and actives sales in your same neighborhood.

4. You will improve. When you are first getting started with repair estimates, it can seem intimidating. However, after doing a few

estimates and using some of the strategies in this book, you become an expert in estimating repair costs.

Even once you gain a level of comfort with estimating repairs, you should always seek out further knowledge through books like this, other real estate investors, training events, talking with contractors, and anything you can do.

There is always something you can learn from other successful investors when it comes to estimating repairs.

5. The fifth thing to keep in mind when doing repair estimates is that this should not take hours and hours. If I am meeting with a seller or walking through a property, it will usually take under 15 minutes. In fact, many times I will just take photos of the property and then go through the repair estimator sheet later filling in the info.

The last thing you want to do is spend hours or days going through your repair estimator before getting back to the seller. If you have a motivated seller, you often times need to make them an offer the same day.

Fortunately, once you get the process down for estimating repairs, you will be able to come up with a number in under 15 minutes.

6. When estimating repairs, you will never be 100% correct, and that is ok. The idea with the repair estimate is to get in the general ballpark of renovation cost. You just don't want to be the investor who is off by 50% on their amount.

    Also, it would be near impossible to be 100% correct on any repair estimate because of all the variables in any rehab. The strategy I use that we will go over in this guide is to use a repair estimator which has about 25 different line items and then to add 10% to the total cost that I come up with.

7. Lastly, you should be using the MAO or maximum allowable offer formula for your offers. Coming up with a repair estimate is

part of the MAO formula and works like this. MAO equals the after renovated value times .7 minus the cost of repairs.

So if a property will sell for 300K renovated and needed 50K worth of repairs, you would take 300K times .7 minus 50K which would give you 160K as the most you should offer for a property.

Okay, so there you have it, seven things to keep in mind when coming up with your repair estimate. In the next section, we go over the three main ways of estimating repairs accurately.

---

3 Ways Of Estimating Repairs

When it comes to estimating repairs, there are really 3 different ways of doing it, some which are better than others. Each method has its own pros and cons which we will go over. The best way is to have a repair estimator sheet, even though some investors prefer to do a cost per square foot average, while others like to do a ballpark lump sum number.

For starters, I would recommend using a repair estimator sheet which you can download for free on my website www.jeff-leighton.com. In another section, we will discuss how you can tell if something needs to be replaced or not, but a general rule of thumb is to err on the conservative side and have it replaced.

The repair estimator is great because it includes all of the major components of a property in a line item format.

In addition, once you fill out the repair estimate, there will be an extra 10% added to the construction costs for overages. And, in almost every scenario, your actual repair cost will be more than your estimate. Keep that in mind and don't be surprised.

The repair estimator helps you get a close estimate, because the last thing you want to do as a newer investor is to be way off with your estimate. Ask me how I know.

You can take the sheet with you when looking at houses or just make a note and take pictures while you are at the property and then calculate everything later. You also should not be spending hours on this document.

In fact, it should be done within the time frame of a simple walk-through of the property. When in doubt, mark the item as needing to be replaced. You will have a pretty good basis for renovation costs after completing this document.

When I was a newer investor, I used to do repair estimate walk-throughs for a more experienced investor who would send me to 10 properties per day.

I would send him my repair estimate sheet as well as any notes, and he would have a great idea of the property condition and repairs needed. After doing a few walk-throughs, you will get it down.

Another way of estimating repairs is on a per square foot basis. When doing a complete gut renovation or building a new construction property, experienced investors tend to do more per square foot estimates. Some investors I know will estimate around 100 up to 150 per square foot for higher-end renovations and new construction in high-end areas.

While this is a viable strategy, I would only recommend this for more advanced investors. The cost per square foot method varies drastically for each area, type of property, level of finishes, and more.

The way most investors come up with their per square foot model is from direct experience of doing numerous rehabs and new construction projects. I would not use this method until you have done numerous deals.

Many investors, including myself, have started with smaller projects and worked their way up to large projects. I also can't emphasize enough that I would not start with a massive project as one of your first couple of deals unless you come from a construction background.

With larger projects, the likelihood of things going wrong is significantly higher. There are also plenty of smaller deals that you can start with to gain experience.

The last way of estimating repairs is to do a ballpark estimate. For example, if you know how much a style of home costs to renovate fully, you can just say that it will be 75K or 50K or 150K. Investors that do a lot of deals often know exactly how much a property will cost without even seeing the inside of the house.

You will learn how to come up with ballpark estimates by talking with other real estate investors at REIA (Real Estate Investor Association) meetings and real estate meetup groups.

This is again an advanced strategy and one that you can still use in some capacity. If you know investors in your area typically spend X amount on a property, you can use that as a reference and then calculate your own estimate with the repair estimate sheet.

Nowadays, while I prefer to see a property in person, I can make offers over the phone because I know exactly how much a house will cost to renovate.

So there you have it, the three main ways of estimating repairs. They can all be used to some extent, but I would recommend that all newer investors use a repair estimator.

Also, when in doubt, ask a more experienced local investor who you know, like, and trust. And don't feel bashful about asking a more experienced investor, they can give you a ballpark estimate.

They usually love to help newer investors who are up and coming because they were in the same position when they began their career.

How To Become A Construction Expert

In the next section, we go over actual estimate ranges for each part of the house so you can have a general idea of costs and come up with an estimate.

That being said, you should always attempt to learn how to estimate repairs and improve your construction knowledge. I learned how to estimate repairs in a few ways, so you will become an expert at repairs in no time.

When I was a rookie real estate investor, I had no idea how much different repairs cost. I didn't know if a kitchen was 10K or 100K since I had heard both estimates at one time or another. If you watch Million Dollar Listing, which is a great show, you might think that a renovation costs 500K, but most likely that is not applicable to your area. In some areas, you can do a full house renovation for less than 50K.

Fortunately, there are simple ways to further your construction knowledge in addition to reading guides like this. The first thing I did was join every single real estate investor association (REIA) and real estate investing Meetup I could. I would make a note to listen and ask other investors what the cost of repairs for different properties was.

The great thing about these meetings is that they always profile local members' deals they have going on and how much they expected to pay in rehab costs vs. how much they actually paid.

Sometimes, the Meetup groups even gather at the property being rehabbed so you can look at the deal in person. Once you hear a few case studies and start talking to other investors at these groups, you will begin to hear trends and ballpark numbers for what it costs to rehab in your area.

This is very helpful and you should make notes of this.

The next best way to learn about construction is to do online research. There are plenty of home repair estimate sites like HomeAdvisor.com and others that will tell you exactly how much the fix will be depending on your zip code.

These sites often give you a low, medium, and high estimate, which can be very helpful depending on the type of neighborhood you are in.

Lastly, if you have built up your list of contractors, which is simple and easy to do and will be covered in a later section of this guide, you should pay them for an hour of their time to walk through a house with you and give you an estimate.

If you have a good rapport with the contractors or know a friend or family member who is a contractor, they will probably do it for free.

Just tell them you are looking to get a better understanding of a property. You can also just take them out to lunch and show them some pictures of a property and get them to give you ballpark prices and ask them what their last renovation projects cost.

If you took a few investors or contractors out to lunch, you would soon have a great idea of good ballpark prices for construction.

So there you have it, in addition to reading this guide a couple of times, you should also use the aforementioned strategies to further your construction knowledge.

Even though I have a lot of real estate investing experience, I still seek out further knowledge and information on construction best practices and prices. You should too.

That being said, you should always attend local investing Meetups to hear what investors are paying for renovations, do your own research online, and take contractors out to lunch or to walk a property or two with them. I've used all of the aforementioned strategies and still do in many cases.

You should never stop learning. In fact, I recently met up with an investor who had almost 20 projects actively going on and who was still asking me questions about real estate investing, even though he was much more accomplished.

Keep an open mind and always look for additional information that can help you become a more informed investor when it comes to repairs or anything else.

Exterior Cost Estimates

In this section, we are going over the main exterior components of a house renovation and what you need to keep in mind when coming up with your estimate. We will go over how to tell if something needs to be replaced versus repaired.

Also, this section will give you real numbers that you can use, including a low estimate and a high estimate, so you have a range to work with. Keep in mind these estimates are for houses under one million.

Once you get in the million-dollar price range, the prices can shoot up because of the size and particulars of a high-end renovation. These are all estimates, so depending on the price range and size of your property, you should decide whether to go with the lower or higher estimate.

1. **Roof:** Roofs can be a significant expense for an investor depending on the complexity of the roof and the size of the house. For a small townhouse, I would not be too worried if the roof needed to be replaced because of the size. However, with a large single-family house, a roof can add up quickly. The way you know you should replace a roof is pretty straightforward.

    There are a couple of things to look for. Is the roof showing signs of the shingles curling, cracking, or does it have missing shingles? Does the roof have multiple layers of shingles? Is the roof covered in moss and does it look deteriorated? If you see these issues, then it probably means you should replace the roof.

    Generally speaking, it is not difficult to determine whether or not you need to replace the roof. Would a reasonable person look at the roof and say it's in good condition or poor condition?

Take a look at your roof in comparison to other roofs in the neighborhood. At the end of the day, when selling your rehab, you want your roof to look the best in the neighborhood, in addition to interior work.

COST ESTIMATE: The cost to replace a townhouse roof would be about 7K. For a larger single-family house or higher-end detached home, you could easily be at 15K or 25K. Estimate 7K-25K. If you are not sure, 10K is a good starting point. The more complicated and the more ridges and structure to a roof, the more expensive it will be.

2. **Gutters:** Next up are your gutters. While you may not think they are that big of a deal, gutters play a big role in preventing water issues and keeping water away from the house. Damaged or hanging gutters are also a massive eyesore and will kill any chances of curb appeal with your property.

How do you know if you need to replace your gutters? Are the gutters sagging and pulling away from the house? Are the gutters dented, bent, or cracked? Are the gutters filled with water or debris and do they generally look like they are in bad condition? Fortunately, gutters are not that expensive to repair or to replace completely.

COST ESTIMATE: I would budget $500-$5000 depending on how many gutters you have and the complexity of the gutter system. Also, many times you may just have to repair the gutters and not replace them.

3. **Siding:** Siding is a repair that can really make the house shine. Generally, you only need to replace siding on older houses. What you need to look for with siding are damaged pieces, outdated colors, and rotting or warped pieces. If there are just a few places that have damage, you may be able to paint and replace those pieces.

However, if your siding looks really old and in bad condition, then plan on a full replacement. One thing to note is that if your house has asbestos siding, then you should plan on paying extra for a company to encapsulate it and properly remove the siding.

Homes from the 1950s can have asbestos siding. Look up a picture online of what asbestos siding looks like. It is very distinctive and easy to recognize.

COST ESTIMATE: Plan on spending 5K-20K for a full replacement of your siding. If it is just missing pieces here and there, then you probably only have to pay a few hundred to a few thousand.

4. **Windows:** Windows are a part of the house that every buyer will look for. You need to make sure the windows are operable and look great. Every now and then, I will buy a rehab where the previous owner updated the windows to nicer vinyl windows.

Generally, though, the windows need to be replaced. Many times, windows are painted shut or cracked in different places. By replacing the windows, you can get more for your house and have the property looking great, even though windows are not cheap.

COST ESTIMATE: I would budget $250-$400 per window for a full replacement with a nice, modern vinyl window.

5. **Exterior Paint:** One of the simplest things you can do to give your house a boost in curb appeal is give it a fresh coat of paint. When deciding on a good paint color, you never want to go too extreme. Instead, go with a nice neutral color.

   I like to drive around the neighborhood and look at the comps online to find a couple of similar houses with attractive exterior paint colors and then decide.

   In fact, that goes for just about every exterior and interior renovation. Just look at which neighbors and comps have the best ideas and then use those for your property.

   COST ESTIMATE: Expect to pay around $2-$3 per square foot for a house. In other words, it would cost about $2,500 to paint the exterior of a smaller, 1200-square-foot home. I would budget $2,500-$7,000 to paint the exterior depending on the size of your house.

6. **Landscaping:** Landscaping is a must for any rehab project. This can make a great first

impression on potential buyers and make your house stand out. Fortunately, landscaping is not a huge investment of time or money.

Just doing the basics such as trimming hedges, mowing the lawn or putting in sod, and adding mulch can have a significant impact. In a later section of this guide, I have a curb appeal checklist with 15 items to keep in mind.

COST ESTIMATE: For landscaping, you can plan to spend at least $1,000 and up to $5,000 depending on the extent of the project and size of the lot. If you need to remove large trees that are right on top of the property, expect to pay several thousand per tree.

7. **Garage:** If your property has a garage, then you need to make sure it is up to par with the rest of the house. There are some simple upgrades that are not expensive and can make your garage stand out. For starters, you should remove all items from the garage and clean it out as much as possible.

Next, you can do this yourself or hire a garage company to put a professional floor coating on the garage floor which acts as a sealant and looks great.

After that, you can paint the garage a nice light color such as white. Lastly, you should replace the garage door if it's in bad condition.

According to Realtor.com, replacing the garage door has the best return on investment of any renovation project, so don't skimp on that.

COST ESTIMATE: A complete garage renovation, including brand new door, floor sealant, interior paint, trashing everything out, and replacing any light fixtures, will cost around $5,000 total. If you are just cleaning out, re-surfacing, and re-painting, then it should be only a few thousand.

8. **Pools:** A pool is one of those amenities that some people love and some hate. It all depends on what part of the country you are in. In my area on the east coast, I rarely come across pools, but in some parts of the country,

pools are everywhere.

If the pool looks like it's in rough c
and has visible cracks, then factor i   ..e
repairs. Many times you don't need to be a
pool expert to know that a pool needs work.

You also might have to replace various types
of equipment for the pool, such as the pump
and heater or re-plastering over leaks in the
pool.

COST ESTIMATE: If the pool looks like it's
in rough condition and has visible cracks,
then it could easily cost a couple thousand
and as much as 5K to get it in working
condition.

9. **Fence:** Having a fence or removing an old
   dilapidated fence can make a big difference
   for curb appeal. There is nothing like a brand
   new fence, and many buyers prefer the
   privacy that comes with a quality fence.

   If the property currently does not have a
   fence, then I would look around at the
   neighbors' houses to see who has the nicest-

looking fence and then model that one.

COST ESTIMATE: While there are different styles of fences, including wood, metal, and vinyl, you should plan on about $10-$15 per linear foot of fence. In other words, for a quarter acre lot of about 200 linear feet, you would be paying around $2K-6K.

10. **Deck:** A deck can be a great selling point to a house. If the home already has a deck, it will most likely need some additional repairs and finishing to be ready for the next buyer. The regulations and code on decks change all the time, and it would be a good idea to get a deck repair company to evaluate the deck.

Typical repairs include staining and sealing the deck with a fresh new coat of sealer, anchoring deck stairs, replacing deck boards, removing popped out nails, and replacing rotten posts.

COST ESTIMATE: Depending on how much work the deck needs, I would estimate $500 to $2,500 to get the deck in good condition. If you are installing a new deck, be prepared to spend 5K for a smaller wood deck up to 20K for a large composite deck. Deck installation is another item that is always on the list of best ROI for renovations when doing a property.

11. **Septic:** If you are further outside of a city, the property might be on a septic system. Before you buy any house with a septic tank, you must get it inspected since they can be costly to replace.

If the property is listed on the market, then the seller will typically have to hire a company to check it out. If I am buying an off-market deal I will usually pay out of pocket to get a septic inspection.

COST ESTIMATE: It's going to cost about $250-$500 for a septic inspection but could save you a fortune. If a septic system is in bad condition it could cost you anywhere from a few thousand dollars up to 15K. And keep in mind, most properties will not be on septic.

If the septic company say it needs a certain number of repairs, then you should put that on the seller to credit you before closing or to have them pay the septic company directly from the proceeds of the sale.

12. **Demo/Dumpsters:** When you buy a house, one of the first things you have to do is trash out the place and start demoing. When working with motivated sellers, I let them know they can leave whatever they want in the house to make it a hassle-free transaction for them.

Fortunately, there are plenty of trash and junk removal vendors. I would recommend getting a couple of quotes and making sure you use a licensed company for liability reasons.

COST ESTIMATE: Depending on whether the place is a smaller condo, a townhome or a larger single-family home, I would estimate $500 up to $3K.

SECTION 5

Interior Cost Estimates

Now that we got the exterior estimates done, let's head inside and run numbers on the interior renovations.

1. **Kitchen:** Kitchen renovations are crucial to selling a property. Sometimes you can just replace the appliances, paint, and add some nice backsplash. However, if the kitchen is completely outdated, you will need to do an entire kitchen renovation.

   Curb appeal, kitchens, and bathrooms are three of the biggest things buyers notice, so make sure to invest some time and money into your kitchen.

If the property is not that old and the kitchen is in good condition then you may just need to do some updates. You want to get an idea of the comps and see what the top selling properties in that neighborhood have sold for and do your renovation accordingly.

COST ESTIMATE: For a small condo, expect to start at around 10K for a full kitchen renovation. The cost goes up to 15K-35K for a single-family house kitchen renovation. Adjust accordingly for the size and price range of your property.

2. **Layout:** If you are rehabbing a property built before 1990, then there's a good chance you may need to open up some of the walls to have a better layout. Buyers these days prefer as much open flow to the house as possible.

What you may not realize is that you are able to open up non-loadbearing walls as well as loadbearing walls when necessary. There are ways of opening up nearly any space. Just make sure you have a licensed and insured contractor. They may need to bring in their architect and engineer to confirm opening up some walls.

COST ESTIMATE: Expect to pay about 2K upwards of 10K to remove a loadbearing wall if the home has several levels. Removing a non-loadbearing wall is relatively simple and should cost less than 1K. Always check with an engineer or licensed contractor before removing any walls, just to be sure.

3. **Bathrooms:** When renovating a house, you must renovate or at least update the bathrooms. Besides the kitchen, the bathrooms also play a big role in any buyer's decision.

At the very least, you should update outdated bath and light fixtures, painting, and putting in a new vanity. And if you are on a tight budget and can only afford to do one bathroom, then make sure you renovate the master bathroom.

Pick designs and finishes that are in line with comparable sales. If you don't specify with your contractor the exact style and photos of what you want your bathroom to look like, they could end up choosing the cheapest Home Depot supplies. Ask me how I know...

COST ESTIMATE: Expect to pay 5K to 15K for a full bathroom renovation. If it's just a half bath, then the costs should only be about $2.5K to $5K.

4. **Flooring:** Flooring can make or break a sale. This is another part of the renovation where you need to stay up to date on what is popular in your area. For example, in some hip, upscale neighborhoods you won't find carpet anywhere. In other areas, it can be more prevalent. Try to match the top-selling comps with the same type of flooring. Do not cheap out on this part.

You should go through the highest sold comparable properties in your area and make a list of what type of flooring they had in different part of the house. Hardwood floors throughout the living area and tile in the bathrooms are usually a good bet, but always check.

You can often refinish older hardwood floors and make them look great. Buyers often appreciate keeping some of the historic charm of an older property.

COST ESTIMATE: Hardwood floors usually cost about $7-$15 per square foot to install. If you are just refinishing the floors, then expect to pay $2-$6 per square foot. Installing tile is similar and will be in the $7-$15 range. If you are replacing carpet, expect to be in the $2-$5 per square foot range.

5. **Drywall/Sheetrock:** Drywall and/or sheetrock repairs are common in most properties. At the very least, you will need drywall patching throughout the property. In some cases, you may need to replace it entirely. Drywall repairs would be considered more of a minor repair than some of the other items we have gone over.

However, you still want to make sure your drywall contractor is a specialist because there is nothing worse than a cheaply done drywall job with the tape exposed and small cracks throughout the finishes.

COST ESTIMATE: Expect to pay around $500 per room if you need to replace the drywall. Most homes however do not need a full replacement unless they are in seriously bad condition. Drywall repair in general is not that expensive and relatively easy for a contractor to do. You should estimate around $50 - $70 per square foot for drywall repair.

6. **HVAC and Hot Water Heater:** It is common on most rehabs that the HVAC and hot water heater are past their useful life expectancy and need to be replaced. This can be a bigger ticket item, especially the HVAC.

   To find out the age of the HVAC and hot water heater, look at the serial number on the units. The 3rd and 4th digit of the serial number is often the year it was installed. For example, if the serial number is 3506XXXX, then the heater was installed in 2006.

   Every unit and manufacturer can vary. If you can't read the number and the system looks old and rusted, then it's a good idea to replace it. Keep in mind that most systems only last about 15 years.

In some cases, with systems less than 10 years old, you may not even need to replace them as long as they are working fine. Instead, you could just get a tune-up from your local HVAC company.

COST ESTIMATE: To replace a furnace and AC unit, expect to pay around $3,500 - $5000 for each. You will spend about 7K-10K for a full HVAC replacement. A hot water heater usually runs around $1K-2K.

7. **Plumbing:** When buying a house, you should assume that every home could use some plumbing updates. There is always preventive maintenance and small plumbing fixes that can be done throughout the property to make sure it's running well.

Some of these include repairing leaky joints, replacing shut-off valves, low water pressure, slow drains, and ensuring the sump pump works. Typically, these are considered normal or standard updates that should not cost you more than a couple of hours of a plumber's time.

In terms of replacing parts or the entire plumbing system, that is something you and your contractor will have to determine. If there are numerous places throughout the house where the plumbing is not working correctly and the house is old, i.e., built before 1950, then the pipes might need to be replaced.

Homes built in the mid-20th century should have exposed pipes in the basement where you can get a good look at them. Sometimes they are in excellent condition, while other times they are clearly not working correctly and you can see visible leaks and corrosion. Additionally, it's not uncommon for vacant properties to have the copper pipes stolen from them.

In either of these scenarios, it's probably best to start over and replace the pipes completely. Again, you only need to replace pipes on older houses. In homes built after 1960 or 1970, you can often just repair them as needed.

Lastly, in some houses, you will need to add a bathroom in the basement or another section of the house. Having enough bathrooms can get you top resale value once the home is renovated. Consider this if your house does not have enough bathrooms.

COST ESTIMATE: Expect to pay $5K-15K to replace the pipes for a large, older house. If you are adding a bathroom in the house, I would factor $5K-20K for a full bathroom installation. If the home is newer, it will most likely only need minor updates and repairs in the ballpark of $1K-5K.

8. **Electrical:** Nearly every house I come across has electrical work that could and should be done. With rehabs you always want to try to add lights when possible and you must also factor in replacing all the switches, outlets, and light fixtures.

Those simple renovations will give your property a much cleaner and more modern look. Additionally, you will want to consider upgrading the service panel if it's 100 amps or less.

Newer homes are built with 200 amp panels,

to give you an idea. Every now and then, you will run across a house that needs to be re-wired entirely, which can get expensive.

There is no real way to tell without bringing in an electrician, but if it's an older house, the electrical panel is a mess, and you see other signs like charred outlets and switches, then you should add re-wiring to the budget.

COST ESTIMATE: Expect to pay $7K-20K to re-wire a house, depending on the size. Keep in mind that the majority of homes don't need to be re-wired. Upgrading the panel is in the ballpark of $2K-3K and can make the house seem much more modern and appealing to the end buyer. The cost of updating and replacing all the outlets, switches, and light fixtures should be in the ballpark of $1,500-$3,000.

9. **Carpentry (Trim and Molding):** To really make your property stand out when you go to sell, the trim work around windows, doors, and moldings should have nice tight sharp corners. This is a simple yet overlooked repair that can give your property that extra boost to

stand out.

COST ESTIMATE: Replacing the trim and molding is in the ballpark of $1K to 5K. If you get really high-end with the crown molding, you can expect double that price.

10. **Termites:** Termites can be an issue in some parts of the country, particularly in the south and southwest. They like wooden structures such as porches, decks, garages, as well as any damp areas near a property.

Since your end buyer will do a termite inspection as a requirement of their loan, you should pay for a termite inspection and do any necessary repairs to be proactive.

COST ESTIMATE: If you need just a basic treatment and repair, expect to pay around $500. However, if there is a larger termite issue, you could spend as much as $2,000-$5,000. In my experience in the mid-Atlantic area, significant termite damage is very rare.

11. **Interior Paint:** The interior of 100% of the houses you buy and renovate will need to be

painted. Always go with a lighter, neutral color. This is not the time to experiment with colors you've never tried before.

Make sure to paint not just the walls but also the ceilings and trim work. This will make your property stand out and show that you don't cut corners.

COST ESTIMATE: Expect to pay around $3-$6 per square foot when you paint the interior of the house. I would highly recommend hiring someone to do this. Just because you painted your room one time does not qualify you to paint an entire house so that you can save a few thousand dollars. Hire a professional and get it done right. It will save you a ton of time and headaches.

12. **Mold:** Mold is another issue you will run into in some properties. Fortunately, mold is typically easier to remediate than most would have you believe. In fact, one of my investor friends preferred to buy houses with mold because it scared everyone away and he knew he could remove it affordably.

Mold is often a result of bad grading on the exterior of the house. The process for removing the mold issue typically involves spraying the areas with mold killer and then cutting any drywall that is affected. Mold removal companies will also have an air filtration vacuum.

After removing the mold, they will either improve the grading with landscaping or in some cases install a French drain or sump pump. In rare cases, a basement waterproofing company will install a full waterproofing system.

COST ESTIMATE: Always consult a professional mold removal company, but expect to pay anywhere from $500 for a little bit of mold up to $10K for serious mold throughout the house. If you are unsure about the mold, then you should probably not buy the house. A full waterproofing system for a basement can run anywhere from $2K to $10K and they typically come with a lifetime warranty.

13. **Permits:** As an investor, you should also

factor in the cost of permits. You should also become well versed in the permit process so that you can get work done quickly and for the best price. The last thing you want to do is ignore permits and try to take shortcuts on the job.

If you have done a significant renovation, the first thing any potential buyer will ask is, what contractor did the work and did they pull permits? You want to be sure you can easily answer that question so make sure to hire a licensed contractor who pulls necessary permits.

COST ESTIMATE: Permits will cost anywhere from $250 up to $3K if there is a lot of work involved. Depending on the scale of your project you should estimate accordingly.

14. **Insulation**: A nice selling feature is having upgraded insulation. Most older homes do not have the proper amount of insulation, and you don't want to have a buyer come back three months after you sold them the house complaining that it's cold. Insulation is also usually easy to install.

COST ESTIMATE: For adding insulation to a property you should factor on at least $500 and upwards of $5000 if it's an older, larger house.

In this section, we covered the main components of any renovation. Like I mentioned, budget on the conservative side if you are not sure. In addition, once we add up our number, we always add a minimum 10% cost to any rehab project, just to be sure.

These estimates will get you right in the ballpark of the actual costs of a project. For older houses or large homes over 4,000 square feet, you will have to keep your budget on the conservative side and add at least 15% to your rehab budget.

SECTION 6

Helpful Rules Of Thumb

In this section, we will go over 9 rules of thumb when it comes to estimating repairs that you must understand. These principles are universally true for a beginner investor or even an experienced investor.

Rule of Thumb #1: For starters, the older the house, the more repairs you will need to do. I know that sounds simple enough, but with older homes, there could be a lot of unknowns that you are not even aware of when you first see the property.

When you open up the drywall, you might find things you were not expecting, like a faulty electrical system, leaking plumbing, and more.

That's why condo fees at older buildings are so high versus newer condos: they have significantly more maintenance to deal with.

Rule of Thumb #2: The next principle is that the larger and more complicated your rehab project is, the more conservative you need to be. There is a big difference between doing a simple townhouse cosmetic fix and flip versus doing a two-story addition on a single-family house and digging out the basement so that it can be finished off.

If you are new to real estate, I would never recommend doing a massive project like that as your first deal just because there is so much more that can go wrong and costs can get out of control.

Always start out with a smaller project and work your way up to large projects. The larger projects should be the most profitable, but you need to make sure you have the experience to take on something like that.

Rule of Thumb #3: Do not rely on estimates from others. If a wholesaler or real estate agent tells you that the property needs only 30K worth of work, make sure you verify that number yourself.

On paper, a deal can look great, but real estate agents and especially wholesalers have a well-deserved reputation for inflating numbers or not accurately estimating repairs.

I am always skeptical of other people's repair estimates and have seen many cases where their estimates are off by more than double. That's not to say there are no good deals from wholesalers and real estate agents. You can find amazing deals, but make sure you always do your own due diligence.

Rule of Thumb #4: When coming up with your repair estimate, always add 10 percent to your grand total. If you want to make profitable deals, then make sure you are adding at least 10 percent to your rehab estimate. The repair estimator I have on my website has that built in and it's a pretty simple formula either way.

Additionally, if you are doing a large project over 100K in repairs, then I would recommend you add at least 15% to your construction budget.

Even after having been in the business for a while, I still add that amount to the total for unexpected costs. Nearly every rehab will have some type of surprise or something you overlooked.

Rule of Thumb #5: Every now and then, you will have to make an estimate on repairs for a property that you have never seen the interior of. I have bought several houses like that, and there are a couple things to keep in mind. You should drive by the outside of the house and try to get a look at the foundation and sides of the house.

Most homes do not have major foundation issues, but usually you can get a good idea of the house just by looking at the exterior. Then factor in that the house will need a full gut renovation. There is a chance that the property won't need that much work, but it's better to stay on the safe side.

Rule of Thumb #6: This is the golden rule of estimating repairs and renovating properties. Always get three bids for your job. I don't care if you have the best contractor of all time. To keep them honest and possibly find a better contractor you always need three bids.

Just make sure they know exactly what you are looking to do because I've seen repair bids come in all over the place when people are not crystal clear about the scope of work they are looking to get done.

Rule of Thumb #7: Use the MAO or maximum allowable offer formula for all of your deals. When getting started in real estate investing, it can be tempting to think every other house that needs work is a good deal. In reality, when you use the MAO formula, you will quickly eliminate about 90 percent of the deals out there.

The MAO formula takes into account your repair estimate and your after renovated value and spits out precisely the number you would need to offer for a profitable deal.

This formula will help you even if your repair estimate is slightly off because of how conservative a number it is. The way it works is you take the after renovated value and multiply it by .7, and then subtract for the cost of repairs.

That number is the most you should pay for a property. So if a property sells for 300K renovated and needs 50K worth of work, you would multiply 300 times .7 minus 50K, and you would get 160K as your maximum offer price.

Although you can go above .7 when it comes to higher-priced homes, I would recommend sticking to this formula until you have built up a lot of experience.

Rule of Thumb #8: When it comes to estimating repairs and the actual construction, your project will cost more and take longer than you were planning. Now, that's not to say that your deals can't be immensely profitable, but it's just something you should expect going in.

Once you get into a rehab, there will be things you might want to do differently or add to the project. That is okay, as long as you plan on some variables before going into the deal.

Rule of Thumb #9: Lastly, when it comes to choosing a contractor for your job, I usually prefer a general contractor. A GC is more expensive than if you just hire electricians, plumber, carpenters, etc., but having a good GC manage the project for you can save you tons of time and headache.

By having a good GC, you can have multiple projects going on at once and not lose your mind. You can consider managing smaller projects yourself, but for larger projects, I would recommend letting the experts handle it.

Repairs That Add the Most Value

In this section, we will go over what repairs add the most value and what you should try to focus on doing. It's incredible to me how some owners will renovate a property only to have it be less appealing than it was before. Focus on these repairs to get the best return on investment.

The first thing you should do is make sure the curb appeal is top of the line. I have been into hundreds, if not thousands, of homes and curb appeal makes a massive difference.

First impressions are everything in real estate. Curb appeal is also easy to implement and not very expensive to do, so there is no reason not to focus on this. Depending on your budget, this is a checklist of items to do for curb appeal. These 15 inexpensive items will instantly give potential buyers a better impression of your property.

1. Mow the lawn and trim the hedges
2. Paint the exterior
3. Plant flowers or put them in flower pots
4. Power-wash your front patio area
5. Clean or replace the windows
6. Replace the entry door or buy an upgraded handle
7. Replace the garage door
8. Install a modern doorbell
9. Ensure gutters are clean and in proper alignment
10. Add upgraded light fixtures in the front-of-house entryway
11. Replace house number
12. Repair/Replace or paint shutters
13. Make sure your walkway is in good condition and repair or add lighting as needed
14. Repaint or replace the mailbox
15. Clean up your yard as much as possible

The next part of your renovation that can give you the best ROI is opening up space as much as possible. For whatever reason, older homes were built with many rooms and walls and can make the property feel much smaller than it is. Have your licensed contractor evaluate and try to open up the space as much as possible.

Many times, it is much easier than you would think to open up a space. Buyers nowadays are looking for open and modern homes. In fact, I just sold a property that I completely rehabbed, but I did not open it up because it was a townhome.

The house next door sold for 30K more than mine and was not even fully renovated, but it was open. That was the main difference buyers were looking for.

The third thing you should focus on is going lighter and more modern. That means nice light neutral paint and floors, as well as focusing on a modern touch throughout with things like light fixtures and door handles.

If you can add more natural light to the property,

then do that as well by replacing older doors or even adding a skylight.

One of my associates just did a small yet impactful renovation on a condo they were selling. It was a condo, so it was not a massive renovation, but it made a big difference and got the property sold quickly when the first listing agent could not sell it.

They replaced the main light fixtures in the unit with brighter and more modern fixtures, installed a modern thermostat, painted the property a lighter neutral color, and replaced the door fixtures with a modern style. All of these inexpensive repairs made the property really pop, and they quickly got an offer and sold it.

Overall, if you focus on curb appeal, opening up space, and then going for a lighter/modern feel, you should be in a great position to get your property sold fast with a nice ROI.

That being said, according to HGTV and Fixr, the top ten home renovations with the best ROI also include kitchen, bathrooms, new windows, new appliances, decks, siding, and roof.

I would recommend focusing on the basics of what buyers are looking for and trying not to do anything out of line with where the neighborhood comps are. Before doing your renovation, you should have a good idea of what different properties in that neighborhood have done and try to model the best ideas that you've seen.

Top Mistakes When Estimating Repairs

There are some common mistakes when it comes to estimating repairs that you must be aware of. I have literally made all of these mistakes, and I can tell you by reading this section thoroughly you will be able to save a lot of money and headaches.

1. The first mistake is that when people are creating an estimate, they are often not aware of the finishes and renovations of similar style homes.

   For example, in some areas, the highest-priced homes might not even be renovated at all. Instead, they might all be in livable condition. That means you might be making a big mistake by doing a full-scale renovation, when instead you could do more cosmetic items and still get a great ROI.

Or for example, in other areas, all of the comps might be very high-end renovations. If you did a middle-of-the-road or low-end renovation, your property would stick out like a sore thumb.

The reverse is true as well. I have seen some investors go into a low-price neighborhood and try to build the Taj Mahal of rehab projects with marble floors and what not.

You can waste a lot of money by going over the top on your project and not understanding what similar properties have done as far as renovations. Make sure to study online or, even better, check out open houses of similar homes in the area to get an idea for your finishes.

2. Another mistake that I wanted to reiterate is

that I see a lot of rehabbers relying on estimates from others, including real estate agents, wholesalers, or even sellers in some cases. Wholesalers will almost always send you a deal that looks great on paper but in reality, their construction numbers can be way off.

That is not to say you can't find amazingly lucrative deals from wholesalers, but take their numbers with a grain of salt.

I've found real estate agent estimates to be much closer, although still a bit lower than the actual estimate. Unless that agent is actively doing deals themselves or unless you have worked with them in the past, then I would always try to verify the numbers yourself.

Most of the time, sellers underestimate the costs of the repairs. Selling a house can be an emotional time, and they might not want to tell you the entire home needs to be renovated.

However, the good thing about repair estimates is that once you do a couple and start doing rehabs, you will soon learn exactly what different styles of properties need without even having to spend too much time.

3. A third mistake I see a lot of newer real estate investors make is that they take forever to come up with a repair estimate. Keep in mind that this is an estimate, not an exact number. The goal is not to be 100% correct; the goal is just to not be off by a significant amount.

   I remember showing a property a while ago to some "investors" who spent almost an hour at the house examining every closet and taking pictures of the landscaping and other trivial items.

   This is a complete waste of time, and an experienced investor would never do this. A repair estimate should be a 15-minute walk-through of the property, noting the items that need work. And if you aren't sure, just take a picture and mark the item as needing to be replaced.

   The last thing you want to do is lose a deal because you took too long to get back to the seller about your offer. Some investors want to get several estimates before even making an offer. Good deals never last, so be sure to do a conservative estimate if you are not sure and get back to the motivated seller ASAP with an offer.

4. While investors tend to underestimate repairs, I do sometimes see newer investors who overestimate repairs. How do I know? Well, when I was getting started, I was on the super conservative side of things and missed out on many great deals because I overestimated repairs.

Here is what I want to tell you. If you are unsure of whether or not a property is a good deal, reach out to a local investor who you know, like, and trust and ask them about their opinion.

Not everyone buys properties to do a complete renovation, so if the property is still priced as one of the lowest comps in the area, then chances are that deal has a lot of potential. More experienced investors might have a large buyers list of local investors that pay a premium for fixer-uppers.

Even to this day, when I'm not sure about the repair costs, I will still partner with a more experienced investor to wholesale the deal to one of their thousands of potential buyers.

5. Just ballparking a repair number. If you are an experienced investor, then you often know exactly how much a property will take to renovate.

However, when getting started, I would be sure to use a repair estimator. If you try to just ballpark a number, you will almost certainly be wrong. Also, a repair estimator only takes a few minutes to fill out and is a helpful tool for anyone.

You would be surprised how many additional items you come up with when you have an actual repair estimator instead of a wild guess. After practicing with the repair estimator on different styles of properties, you should start to get an intuitive feel for how much a property will cost.

How To Find
The Best Contractors

In this part, we will go over how to find the best contractors for rehabbing houses. Keep in mind that you should be aiming to build a list of good contractors instead of just finding one good contractor. Most investors are not strategic with making their list of contractors.

Sometimes contractors get busy with other projects, sometimes your contractor's quality of work may start going down, and you always need three bids on a project. Therefore, it's essential to have an "all-star" team of contractors. These strategies should make it fairly easy for you to create a list of at least 10 qualified, pre-vetted contractors.

1. My favorite way of finding contractors is simple and easy. Drive around in the neighborhood where you have bought a property or where you will be buying a property and look for contractor yard signs.

   I see countless yard signs and contractor trucks with the contact information of the company in just about any neighborhood I go to.

   When you see these, you can write down the number and website and start building a list. You could quickly create a list of 5-10 contractors with this strategy alone.

   It's a good sign when a contractor is working in your neighborhood since they will know those types of properties. Plus, you should be driving around the neighborhood anyway to get a good feel for the comps.

2. The next way to add names to your list of contractors is to ask for referrals from friends,

family, real estate professionals, co-workers, and anyone else you can think of. People love recommending contractors if they did a great job. Sometimes they even go in depth to show you the before-and-after photos of the work they had done.

3. The websites of local real estate agents are another great resource. What you can do is look up different real estate agents in your city and go to the "recommended vendors" or a similar section on their websites.

   They will have a list of recommended title companies, lenders, and also contractors. While not every agent will have this, many of the top agents in your area should have a list of contractors they like to use. By just spending an hour or so online, you should be able to add even more qualified contractors to your list.

4. Another great way to find contractors is through Angie's List and Yelp. Angie's List is great because you can sign up for free and find discounted deals on contractor services as well as all the reviews from people who

have used that service.

Angie's List also does a great job of prescreening the contractors for you. Yelp is not as good as Angie's List, but it's a good idea to check the Yelp reviews as well. Some contractors may not have Yelp, but I would still check. You want all the available information on a contractor.

5. Home Depot and other supply houses. If you go to Home Depot, Lowes, as well as specialty supply stores for electrical, HVAC, plumbing, and others you can ask for recommended contractors.

    The people at these stores should have no issues whatsoever recommending a few names to you. In fact, they should be happy to do so. It would only mean more business for them as well, since the contractors frequent their stores.

6. Lastly, you should be attending REIA (real estate investor association) meetings as well as real estate investing Meetup groups in your area. At these events, there will probably be

contractors whose contact information you can get.

Additionally, you can ask other investors there if they have any recommended contractors. They will probably give you recommended contractors as well as contractors to avoid.

These strategies should make it easy for you to build a list of at least 10 qualified, recommended contractors – if not 25. Keep in mind that some contractors might not be available all the time, so you need to have a large qualified list.

Before you pick your contractor, remember a few things. The best contractors are always busy, so you should be a little hesitant if the contractor does not seem to have too much going on.

Next, make sure your contractor is licensed and insured, which is something they should provide easily to you. Lastly, even after you have your qualified list of great contractors, you should still get three bids just to make sure everyone is on the same page.

And while nothing is ever guaranteed, by using those strategies to find contractors, you will maximize your likelihood of doing a successful rehab.

Now It's Your Turn

Thanks for reading this guide. You should now have everything you need to start making educated estimates on construction repairs for your deals. Keep in mind that you will never be 100% correct on the estimate, but it will help you get right in the ballpark of the actual costs. I see far too many investors making uninformed estimates because they don't know any better.

I hope that you enjoyed this informative guide. I have tried to add as much value as possible.

If you enjoyed this book and found it useful, I'd be very grateful if you would leave an honest review. Every review makes a difference, and I read and appreciate all feedback.

Thanks again,

Sincerely
Jeff Leighton

About The Author

Jeff Leighton is a real estate investor, real estate broker, and bestselling Amazon Author. He has been mentored by some of the top real estate investors in the US and continues to invest in real estate to this day.

Want More Training?

Go to www.jeff-leighton.com for helpful videos, free resources, downloads, additional mentoring, online programs, and much, much more. You can also text **DEAL to 345345** to stay updated on everything we have going on in the real estate investing world.

Other Books By The Author

Available on Amazon

Follow Jeff Leighton

Instagram.com/J_Late12
YouTube.com/JeffLeighton1
Facebook.com/JeffLeighton5

Made in the USA
Middletown, DE
02 January 2020

82430913R00046